Rain; road;
an open boat

BOOKS BY ROO BORSON

Rain; road; an open boat (2012)

Personal History (2008)

Short Journey Upriver Toward Ōishida (2004)

Introduction to the Introduction to Wang Wei
(with Pain Not Bread) (2000)

Water Memory (1996)

Night Walk: Selected Poems (1994)

Intent, or the Weight of the World (1989)

The Transparence of November/Snow
(with Kim Maltman) (1985)

The Whole Night, Coming Home (1984)

A Sad Device (1981)

Rain (1980)

In the Smoky Light of the Fields (1980)

Landfall (1977)

Rain; road;
an open boat

ROO BORSON

McClelland & Stewart

LIBRARY AND ARCHIVES CANADA CATALOGUING IN PUBLICATION

Borson, Roo, 1952–
Rain, road, an open boat / Roo Borson.

Poems.
ISBN 978-0-7710-1298-3

I. Title.

PS8553.O736R35 2012   C811'.54   C2011-904426-9

Published simultaneously in the United States of America by McClelland & Stewart Ltd., P.O. Box 1030, Plattsburgh, New York 12901

Library of Congress Control Number: 2011931128

We acknowledge the financial support of the Government of Canada through the Book Publishing Industry Development Program and that of the Government of Ontario through the Ontario Media Development Corporation's Ontario Book Initiative. We further acknowledge the support of the Canada Council for the Arts and the Ontario Arts Council for our publishing program.

Typeset in Aldus by M&S, Toronto
Printed and bound in Canada

ANCIENT FOREST
FRIENDLY

This book was produced using recycled materials.

McClelland & Stewart Ltd.
75 Sherbourne Street
Toronto, Ontario
M5A 2P9
www.mcclelland.com

1   2   3   4   5   16   15   14   13   12

CONTENTS

RAIN

> The narrow
> guest bed –
> what will you dream?

The honey-coloured light in the pines, the faint sound of surf from the other side of the house. Through the winter months the house is rented out. This is the moment chanterelles and boletus come up – come up after the light summer rains. Lie down with your face toward the window then. One wall is all windows, and in the windows, this room –

≈

At that place where the river widens, spilling out over sand to the ocean, there's a shack, painted grey. A few tables and stools, a counter, the listing of twelve or so kinds of sausages the years have not changed. Bratwurst. Polish. Garlic. Etc. The whole place has a clean-washed feel, and disappears into the fog, or else melds with the silver-plated sky.

> A face comes back
> this summer day
> so like her

Melds with the silver-plated sky after rain so it's hard to find without a map, though where the river road meets with the coast road, that's where you'll find it.

≋

All night the scrabblings of mice in the attic have sounded, now reckless, now surreptitious, until with the first pre-dawn light the spell is broken, and one by one they drop off to sleep once more. Now it is the turn of the things in the kitchen to stand out: the beautiful old floorboards, a plate painted in 1937 upright in the dish-rack, the year too painted in gold on its back. Out the window hummocks and windrows blush maroon, the long spindles of the rising sun bringing back the familiar autumn world. Overnight a water strider has died in the bucket, two flies on the windowsill. *Err on the side of kindness,* say the last words of a dream – advice that should be simple enough to follow, in a place where the stove is named Coquette, and the radio Symphonaire.

≈

Once or twice a year I visit what was once my home. Often the roof is missing, along with some or all of the walls, which is only to say that the house is never quite the same from one visit to the next. No matter what time of night I arrive the house is full of people, none of whom I've seen before. Still, there's always plenty of room, and a place can be found for me should I decide to stay. Of course the property itself has changed hands several times. This was after the old house burnt down, though before the new one, monstrous as it is, was built to take its place. Yet even so the old house remains. And the older woman who was my mother – that woman, along with the magnolia grandiflora and two double purple wisterias brought all the way from China, is still there, alive at the root.

≈

The Botanic Garden is situated right beside the cancer clinic of the city's largest public hospital. It's common to see people in nightgowns, pyjamas, fluffy slippers, all manner of intimate dress here, walking the paths. On any given day you might see a person half leaning on, half pushing their own oxygen module on a portable dolly, hospital gown gaping open at the back, or perhaps catch a glimpse of a red-haired woman in a white satin bathrobe strolling, eyes straight ahead, through the cactus garden. Today a young man has been wheeled down the lawn in his hospital bed, to the very edge of the lotus pond. The blossoms and leaves long gone, his friend stands behind him, arms leaned along the headboard, brown stems and seed pods making wiry shadows on the blanket of autumn duckweed.

≈

After lunch we go walking. It has rained a lot lately, and red ants are busily climbing in and out of nipple-holes in the bare dirt. One bears forward a golden inch-long lance, without stumbling. Farther off, station wagons and ranch-style houses, the usual clouds massing toward the mountains. Together we identify alfalfa and mallow, sage and Indian paintbrush. I'd long since forgotten the name of the elegant, taller grass with the feathery seed-head shaped like an old-fashioned razor, but this morning I awoke early, troubled by the words "grama grass." The living bark of the ponderosa pine smells like vanilla, but you have to go right up to it, you have to lay your head against the bark to smell it.

≈

Tufts from the cottonwoods, set loose in the world. They drift among the trunks, turn, hesitate, seeking sunlight or shade, alight in the rushing foam, in the hair of those who walk beside the river. The river is full this year, more rain than anyone can remember. Someone stands motionless holding out a fishing rod. At the head of San Francisco Street, the cathedral, in whose monumental stillness shadows fall, or memory lengthens – the high facade, the small round windows through which light is channelled inward, bathing rejoicers and mourners alike.

≈

One day we go walking, a friend and I, down through Cedarvale Ravine, then east along the Beltline Trail, crossing over Yonge Street via the footbridge, with the subway tracks below. We've been this way before, though never this far: all the way to the Davisville gate of the Mount Pleasant Cemetery, where the crypts of the wealthy weigh down the earth. I could always move in early, jokes my friend, and indeed each miniature mansion of solid stone has a door but no windows, and looks just big enough for a person to live in. Drag in an old mattress and a teakettle, I say – I'm following his line of reasoning – but no, he replies, he'd be content just to sleep on the floor. It's a beautiful day. Rashes of bluebells beneath the trees, the gnarled old pines in sturdy shapes, and a hawk sailing high over it all.

≈

> One string of morning glories,
> a pen for holding cattle –

Our room in the guesthouse is decorated with this couplet, something taken from a famous poem. A length of silk morning glories has been pressed behind glass and framed, and the words are written in the lower right-hand corner of the picture. Poetry is part of the decoration, part of the daily life here. I've seen this poem before but no longer know who it's by – Li Bai, perhaps, or could it be Han Shan? Han Shan is less famous here than in the West. In the poem it's not yet spring, but in our room it's the night of the Mid-Autumn Festival: mooncakes have been left for us to mark the celebration. In fact the moon itself is visible, rare in Beijing, the colour and shape of an apricot, rising through the smog.

> Night sky tonight –
> pen holding the moon

For each of us, there is a place from which our night-dreams proceed and around which our mental faculties take shape. Mine lies along the coast between Point Arena and Gualala, at a particularly deep turning of the road. In the shadow of two hills and shrouded by redwoods, this place remains dark and cold even in summer. If you stop at this point and walk several paces into the woods, you'll be rewarded with the sight of a tree not native to these parts, one belonging to the mountains farther south, or else farther in the past or future. Unremarkable looking, it is a sparse flat-needled evergreen whose bark, used as a medicine, cures certain ills, while at the same time causing others. Related to the Pacific yew, whether as remnant or harbinger, as you are, in kind, to your own distant relatives, it bears neither cones (as such) nor readily edible fruit, and makes itself at home wherever it happens to issue from the earth.

WILD VIOLETS

Morning on the road to the coast,
the past —
but who could live there?

Each year sounding
that much more devoted,
the young whippoorwills.

Rainy day bath —
a stray hair
makes the letter $\mathcal{L}$.

Recovering the chair cushion I remember
when I wore that dress
last I was fourteen.

Early to bed,
moonlight
afloat in the trees.

Hers or
mine? White hairs clinging to
what used to be my mother's sweater.

Walking in
with a bucket of mussels
and a crooked smile, "Here's lunch!" she says.

Surf whitens –
dog barking –
sun just down.

Dog barking,
late into the evening.
Everywhere, long summer shadows.

After fifty years
to come upon them here again: forget-me-nots
in the margins of the grass.

Black moth
beside my black sock.
Happiness at last!

Clearing out the house
I find
old papers dog-eared in a closet.

"Wild violets in the salad – !"
in a
letter never sent.

RADISH FLOWERS

In deepening shade
the scent of wild radish flowers
first summer day

There beneath the huckleberry bush
a shrew's skull
early dawn

Trying to finish
one more page
moths by lamplight

Stumbling about on the wooden deck
my heart past midnight
deer or something else there

The neighbour's orange trumpet vine
suddenly today the old fence
poking through it

A sprinkle of rain on the roof
forlorn now
and the smell of mouse droppings

Rainy day beach
bloodworms like veins in sand
distant horizon

A raccoon's death
to be in the world but not of it
sunlight on the autumn highway

One June we stayed in one of the row houses located on the edge of a stretch of woods just up the hill from the porter's office on the grounds of Grey College at the University of Durham. By day I would pass that office on my way downhill and into town, where I'd buy muffins, cheese, and beer, then lug them back uphill again. In Durham is one of the great cathedrals of England. It stands on the banks of the River Wear, and can be seen from many places in the city. Sometimes, passing nearby, I might hear a choir singing, the sound as if warmed in its passage through the old stone walls. Not far from the college the city gives way to patches of forest and countryside. For a full week the woods were bathed in a blue light, the light of bluebells which had bloomed there in their thousands. At breakfast-time and dinner-time, rabbits large and small would suddenly appear, either to work at digging holes or play at chasing games, in and out among the hedges. One night I woke up in the pitch-dark. Outside was a birdsong I'd not heard before. Again the next night it was there. Only on the third night, as the song was dwindling, did an old tune, suddenly remembered from some decades earlier, come back, to tell me what it was that I'd been listening to. Waking again some hours later, I could see the first light's elongated shadows stretching out into the green woods. A light rain had been falling, and the trees gleamed, as if newly lacquered. The blackbird is named in that song and, only because of this, named by its own. The shape of a song it seems, even an old one, can't be contained by its beauty alone.

There's a place in the woods, an old abandoned building site, so overgrown it's hard to find. We used to lie on our backs on the cold foundation to look up at the stars: it made a house-sized clearing in the night sky, the posts reaching up straight and sound. From there we could watch the late-summer meteor showers, or fog blowing across the face of the moon.

We knew only that the older, cramped house where the couple had lived was farther down in the forest, at the end of a gravel drive, and that this would have been the new house. Nothing but a foundation and a few posts – but their hopes had already moved there. The posts still smelled of new wood, as though the builder might return at any moment and begin where he had left off.

When the wife died the builder, who was also the husband, sold the property, the new house along with the old. It was a fine place to watch the stars, one of those places where the future seems to open out endlessly. Anyone going there would feel it, no matter their age or in what way their own hopes had been disappointed. I wonder sometimes what's become of it. Thirty years ago all traces of the road to the new house had already disappeared, and sturdy young saplings had taken root all around.

Morning, and the road to the coast.
The past.
But who still lives here?

Rainy day, and so a bath.
A stray hair
makes the letter *L*.

Whippoorwills.
An old dress just remembered
used once for the cushion of a chair.

Early to bed, early to rise.
Dream of moonlight
floating through the trees.

White hairs clinging to
what used to be my mother's sweater.
Hers or mine.

Walking in with a bucket of mussels,
and that crooked smile, she says
"Here's lunch" again.

Surf whitens,
dogs barking,
sun just down.

Late into the evening,
summer shadows
falling in the margins of the grass.

After fifty years
to come upon them here again –
old papers dog-eared in a closet.

Written in an antique hand
"Wild violets in the salad – !"
in a letter never sent.

RAIN; ROAD

Thin sun,
thin rain,
the blossoming oats –

The pale oats were shining, and the sun emerged from beyond the clouds – hanks of pine hair were strewn about, blue with rainwater after the storm. I took the long way round, past the pond where children like to gather, tossing bread to the ducks, the heavy carp, and the turtles, all swimming about helter-skelter, over and under one another, vying for a piece. One of the turtles, an old one, green pond weeds streaming from its back, happened to look up into my eyes with its yellow eyes. We stayed like that, the turtle hanging in the water, me leaning over the railing, old face to old face, until without thinking I reached up to pull off my hairband – and at that it dove like a stone.

≈

To look for the names of people one has known (today on the internet, for example) and find the entries waxing and waning, continuously woven and pulled apart, woven and pulled apart, as though bestowed with a kind of afterlife that is very frail. To see the name of a dead person appearing in this way, especially one who died before this vast burgeoning of facts and fictions that can no longer be distinguished, one from the other, from the truth – but then again, to find only the few stubborn entries, all that remains . . .

≈

A dozen fish laid out side by side, from the largest to the smallest, along the grassy verge of the river, the longest the length of my arm from elbow to fingertips, the smallest no bigger than my hand. Who would do this? Each with several deep maroon gashes in the bluish-silver scales, a few curious native bees weaving back and forth above the blood-filled wounds.

≈

The world in old photos,
or the world in spring –
which is younger?

≈

Each spring in this house comes the first morning when, first thing, without fail, the year's first millipede is sighted, frantically swirling around and around in the dry bathtub or the kitchen sink. Once again (no matter how many times it's happened before) I'm caught unprepared, catapulted briefly into mute terror. And from that day forward, in this house, it's summer.

≈

A novelist I know once said he wouldn't know what to do if he had to take off all of his masks. Another, writing her memoirs, had the feeling she was borrowing someone else's instruments. Are these the same problem, or different problems?

≈

According to the poet Miriel Lenore, to cure an ailing ginkgo tree you should water it with milk. According to another friend, squirrels and rats, rodents in general, absolutely can't stand the smell of human hair. Similarly, according to the next-door neighbour, skunks and onions.

≈

Having been told at different times in my life that I am gifted, stupid, beautiful, homely, have perfect pitch and a tin ear, I've now begun to wonder on what grounds anyone's opinions can be taken seriously. But then this is the opinion of a person who is gifted, stupid, beautiful, homely, with perfect pitch and a tin ear –

≈

There should be a plant whose common name is False Patience. And another called False Promise. Maybe the most delicately structured of the thus-far unnamed common plants, one with feathery fronds and tiny yellow flowers, should be called False Premise. How beautiful it would be, now that spring is here, to walk through a meadow rife with False Start.

≈

As for people, as soon as the reputation outgrows the person, that reputation, or that person, will be stunted for life.

≈

A beautiful little honeyeater, sprawled over on its side, no apparent injury, as though the day's heat alone may have killed it. Thirty-eight degrees. A great swirl of sugar ants beginning to mass beneath it. The eye still open, a clear olive green, matching the patch on its wing. Beautiful little eye, still open on the world.

≋

Once, on a winter night, I woke up to use the toilet, and on my way back to bed glanced out the window. There, along the bare branches of the neighbour's old cherry tree, perched comfortably above the silently glowing snow, were four – four! – of the neighbourhood cats. A fifth, the biggest of the tomcats, slowly stretched his body partway up the trunk, head bowed, apparently asking in this way to be admitted to the upper branches. I thought to myself: I should get out the camera and take a picture of this amazing scene. And in the next moment I thought, sleepily: next time this happens I'll get out the camera and take a picture of this amazing scene – and with that I went back to bed.

≋

Time, it seems, is the one true dimension, the one in which things can arrive and depart. (This according to a friend, not seen for years now.)

≋

Sitting in an armchair in the old nurses' quarters of the Royal Adelaide Hospital on a day of forty-degree heat, reading Edward Seidensticker's *Genji Days* in the racket of the old air conditioner, I come upon the entry for Tuesday, August 7, 1973: "Dinner at Juanita Vitousek's, down on a moonlit beach beyond Diamond Head. . . ." But I know this place! It is Aunt Juanita's house, where my brother first learned to climb coconut palms, knees and elbows bent out to the sides, coconut knife between his teeth. How strange to come upon one of one's earliest memories, far from home, and in the work of a man one has read for decades, yet never met.

≋

A scene remembered from a movie – or else from a dream, recounted by a friend some years ago and now entangled with it. A woman steps into a pharmacy, presumably to fill a prescription, only to find that all four walls are taken up with shelves, each filled entirely with large, old-fashioned glass jars, of a kind once found only in candy shops, containing objects which, though tantalizing in their near-familiarity, in the end remain unrecognizable. Today, out walking, a sign I'd not encountered previously –

Dream Mart!
Grand Opening Soon!

– along Bloor West, near Christie, recalls this scene for me.

≋

According to an old fable, at the point of death, just before crossing over, we will each be allowed to ask, and receive answers to, three questions about the world from which we are about to depart. Any three questions, but no more. For example (so I thought to myself before opening my eyes), you could ask who it is that cut the stairs into the bare rock of Huangshan, or the meaning of that word you'd always meant to look up but could not remember when a dictionary was near, what exactly is the colour red, or who your parents' parents' parents were. But no, no matter how numerous your questions, the strict limit is three, and only the first three, even if one or two slip out inadvertently, are to be answered. If you're to die in your sleep, the answers will be given in a dream.

≋

I went for a walk just as the rain let up. On the wet pavement a white moth, an inch long, a sketchy charcoal stripe decorating the edge of each wing. I crouched down. The battered edge of one wing was still vibrating – and on the head, a perfectly groomed mane of white hair.

≈

It's a common experience in older age to realize that the future one was warned of as a child has finally arrived. It's a peculiar feeling, and arrives with peculiar force: that the present is all that remains of whatever was hoped for, feared, fought over, gained, lost. And now there is only this world, which "that" world has become.

≈

At the same time, history presses closer. Whatever might once have perplexed, or dazzled, with its remoteness, is now taken for granted, having become as natural and familiar as your own skin. So it is today, gazing out an eighth-floor window of the Chang Feng Holiday Inn, the haze of smokestacks combining with sand blowing in from the Gobi Desert to blur the western hills.

≈

From somewhere or other my mother acquired a Chinese kingfisher feather necklace. Kingfisher feathers of this type are an intense turquoise blue and highly prized, and for this reason the species, if indeed still extant, is endangered. She passed the necklace down to me, and from that time it has been kept, along with various papers, in a safe deposit box in a bank vault in downtown Toronto. From time to time, when for one reason or another I go to consult one of the documents in that box, I also take a moment to unwrap the tissue paper and gaze once more on the feather necklace, which is disintegrating at an alarming rate. Disintegrating is the wrong word. Actually it is vanishing from the edges in, eaten away by mites so small they can't be seen with the naked eye.

≈

Of course no one remembers their own birth or death. Others remember for us. Everyone likes to hear the story of when and how they were born. As for the face of the dead person, it is a mirror for our own feeling, which is why witnesses can disagree over the facts, even as to the exact nature of the expression left on the face of one who has just died.

≈

The delicate scent of bottle-gourd blossoms,
the wisteria beans long and flat,
the repetitive songs of the birds of early summer.

≈

Let's say, for argument's sake, that home is the place you longed to get away from, which you long to return to once you can no longer do so. Nostalgia, then – the feeling of being at home in the past even as you live day to day like anyone else – becomes a form of greed. Much later, as we begin to lose our grip on life, there are those among us who are naturally drawn nearer day by day to a past that is more and more remote. But do memories return to us? Or are we returned to them?

≈

Seen once, in a museum, embroidered on a pillow: "Be unconscious of wealth and honour, be awake and careless of the times."

$$\approx$$

Among my closest friends is one who could be described as chronically ecstatic. His enthusiasms know no bounds, and especially he is apt to invest particular artworks with a significance well beyond their common value, speaking of them knowledgeably, reverentially, and at the same time lightheartedly, in this way gradually restoring significance to the world.

$$\approx$$

An everyday game, played once for four days running on a trip across the continent: think of ordinary words which, when capitalized, make plausible-sounding but unorthodox, even rude, girls' or boys' names. This game gave the youngest of my aunts much pleasure in her later years.

$$\approx$$

Another game for travelling the highways: using local place names taken from mileage signs, make up names for fictional characters that give the flavour of the region you're travelling through. One rule: you can't change the order of the names as they appear on a given sign, nor can you combine names from different signs. In the old car's glove compartment, or else in a drawer of the long table, there must still be sheets and sheets of paper bearing wonderful names for characters in novels that will never be written.

$$\approx$$

Standing on the right foot,
lifting pine seeds with the left –
cockatoo etiquette.

≈

People make inferences about other living people using a few indispensable stereotypes which they carry about with them wherever they go. For example, a businessman will be clean-shaven and unscrupulous, a mother obtusely sentimental about her offspring, while a poet will exemplify, simultaneously, simple-mindedness and otherworldliness. It's almost impossible to disabuse anyone of these.

≈

A final variation for whiling away the hours: find a Shakespearian (or other) quotation applicable to a given town name along the highway. For example the town of Ault, off State Road 14, between Pierce and Eaton, Colorado: "Ault! Who goes there?"

≈

Some people are so inclined to envy that they are capable of being envious of other people's happiness – even when the putative cause of that happiness would not have the same effect in them. (When you think about it, most types of envy are sub-types of this one.)

≈

A narrow mind will find a way to shrink the world. But can a broad mind widen it?

≈

A magpie lark
standing guard over the waterfall,
water gliding past its feet –

≈

To rely on the executors of one's will to do one's bidding in every respect
after one's death must be the last resort of foolishness. The farther
from the date of death the farther things stray from one's intentions,
whether of their own accord or due to wilfulness on the part of others.
In fact, this is a principle that holds true even in one's life.

≈

A cathedral; a palace; a mansion. A grand hotel. A shack. A shack blown
down by the wind.

≈

Near tears, saying goodbye for another year to a friend at the station,
when suddenly something flashes past – a pigeon, flying back to join
its mate on a roof-beam. Then there are tears.

People meeting and parting,
birds returning to the roost,
all beneath the station roof –

≈

Nowadays when I look in the mirror I no longer see myself as I once did. A face is there, to be sure, though it is no longer mine except in the provisional sense, belonging instead to a particular long line of faces dispersed across time and a wide arc of the Pacific archipelago.

≋

Cathedral, palace, mansion, hotel, shack blown down by the wind. (One's art, too, has been all of these.)

≋

(And if the place of art, too, should prove to be illusory?) To have lived here, even for a while – !

≋

That time of day when you step out. and the crickets have begun a light music under the fallen leaves, and a stranger you've encountered irregularly over the years, walking the same path in the opposite direction, and with whom lately (speaking in terms of years) you've begun to exchange a shy, acknowledging smile – that stranger is just this moment passing by –

≋

The ruined Corinthian columns of goldenrod, dazzling yellow, of unequal heights, encircled by bees – late sunshine, time incarnate, the continuous flowering of all that exists.

≋

There is a place called White Duck Narrows, where a wooden footbridge links the two banks near a turning in the river. Crossing from one side to the other you can often spot the small flock of ducks that has made this bit of river their evening resting place. This year a perfectly white duck has joined them, presumably a stray, or escapee, from someone's backyard. Looks aside, it appears entirely at ease among them, feeding and swimming, diving and sunbathing on the rocks, chewing the bankside grass. At the same time it seems always to be holding back, following, never leading, the others in their peregrinations – though this interpretation could be no more than misdirected sympathy on my part, an after-effect of seeing its small round eyes peering out of a face that is otherwise blank, as compared with the marvellous scroll-like markings of the others. And then, for two days in a row, finding only a few white feathers drifting on the current, it suddenly occurred to me (perhaps unjustly) that the wild ones must have closed ranks. Just this afternoon, in an unrelated incident, I saw quite clearly two wild ducks from a separate group downstream following in close convoy a magpie goose (which, as you know, is an entirely other species), the trio hastening one after another with great serenity and style down the centre of the river.

Some say the sky is the last great wilderness.
But the last great wilderness

has always been the one just outside this door.
Never since the birth of the first person

has there been such a wilderness.
That person was never born.

The flowers we call baby blue eyes
can't even see us, so small and blue,

their blueness is lost in the meadow. Some
say the sky

is the last great wilderness,
that never since the birth of the first person

has there been a wilderness
that person was never born into,

a door so small and blue
the flowers can't see into it,

lost and not lost,
at home in the marvellous,

in the meadow's unbreakable blue.

One day in the ravine near my house I looked up into a sky so blue it was as if a door had opened into another world. When I looked down again I noticed that baby blue eyes were blooming everywhere in the as-yet-uncut grass. Facing the sky again, standing amongst those flowers, that hidden near-mirror symmetry seemed a formal demonstration, a proof, as it were, in a style of logical argument now long obsolete.

In one corner of the room, beneath the open window, lies an unabridged dictionary becalmed on its stand. Pressed between its pages are buttercups, sage blossoms, several summers' lavender and rose petals, even a small moth that fluttered in haphazardly one evening just as the book was being closed. These mementoes have stained the pages brown, becoming light and friable, more insubstantial over time. The book itself is a code, a key, a lock, an implement that stands for an earlier time and other customs, containing only those things that need not exist, but do so nonetheless, carrying them forward as a maple seed is carried forward by the wind.

In the golden tent
of early morning

when the sky has turned its back
and isn't listening

when the scallops stand upright
on their hinges

in a metre of gentle water
and the ray that flapped from the

waves at midnight now beneath the sand
is sleeping

And with a sky that is always turning
and the ray that sleeps beneath the sand still sailing

and the scallops that stand upright in that gentle water
and the sky that

turning does not listen
and those bells

that are no more between Ardrossan and the point
still pealing

and the morning that was black and without stars
and now is golden

Black Point is a small point of land on the east coast of the Yorke Peninsula in South Australia. It has been known for years for the excellent fishing, including night-fishing, which takes place along its shores, as well as for the numerous, somewhat dilapidated beach shacks, many of which have now been replaced by high-priced vacation properties. The land being quite flat and sandy, the sunrise here has a special diffuse clarity about it. It's the sort of place a group of friends might have made a trip to long ago, remembering such details only now, when one of them has died, giving a definition to what once seemed so far into that future as to be unknowable.

On a day long ago, which is to say no more than a few decades past, when the great age of books had not yet begun to dwindle into that ever-diminishing present we now seem to find ourselves encumbered with, I went walking up a country road where I often liked to walk, sometimes in the morning, sometimes later in the afternoon. The road curved away as it always did, first to the right, then to the left, beneath tall pines festooned with lichen. It was a time when one might be invited in for tea at a stranger's house and stay the night; when sunlight having pooled deliberately around a bookshelf, a book might open with a puff of mildew, the result of fog and the winter rains settling in its pages; when one might read by the firelight given off by the crackling branches of a tree felled some months previous by lightning or the softly hissing pith of another that had fallen of old age. That day, which was actually many days, was one of deep blue skies, of sounds heard on those walks that, heard, last even to this day, caught in those books, beneath that sky –

> The roaring
> high up in the pines
> there is another world

ROADS IN THE BERKELEY HILLS

That night we spent
on a blanket in the hills

the hay weighted down in the wet
the bright-eyed brambles

that have come back now –
as if to say:

that city
which does not exist here any longer

is
inside you

in the smell of eucalyptus
and the bright straw-coloured slopes

the fog that
tumbles up the hills again

*I went back home to visit an old friend, having learned that the
circumstances of his life had changed very greatly – as, I thought, had
mine. Although he was the one to have eventually settled in our old
hometown and I was the one to have left, and though one of his parents
was still alive while mine had both been dead for many years, my life,
it seemed, in comparison, was much as it had always been. Back when
we were still living in the same city we could not have foreseen even*

an inkling of all that would take place. But now, meeting each other again, it was clear that our paths had never once diverged, not even for an instant.

RAIN; ROAD; AN OPEN BOAT

It had begun raining in Seattle as we prepared to depart from that city, and now, some twenty hours later, not long after our arrival in Nara, as if to welcome us back into its domain, all at once the rain continued. The crossing of the Pacific, the onward flight from Tokyo, the bus ride from Osaka lay behind us. Taking shelter from the sudden downpour, we saw something swift and white dart across the park at a distance in front of us and disappear along a line of cypresses.

> In the old world's rain
> the camellia buds'
> new world
>
> Rain jumping like minnows
> among the trees
> enough for ten ponds
>
> Who you are now you were
> even yesterday
> the statues in the park
>
> The king deer
> standing upright
> lightning seen from miles away
>
> If we can't go we'll stay here
> rain pavilion
> resounding in the rain

The next morning, my travelling companion having other matters to attend to, I decided to climb Wakakusa, the local mountain. A wide even path led uphill beneath the still-glistening trees, and every so often a sign was posted warning the visitor not to depart from this path, as the surrounding forest was not to be disturbed. Along the way I passed several other walkers, each of whom nodded a friendly greeting, and after a couple of hours came to within sight of the peak, which looked to command a three-hundred-and-sixty-degree view – only to find it cordoned off with ceremonial ropes. At the same time the weight of the camera I'd felt tugging at my coat pocket all morning long turned out to be that of a book I'd brought along to read on the flight and already finished. The city lay spread out below, a plain of dampened concrete and glass, while nearer to hand tall end-of-summer grasses swayed against the darker colours of the adjoining hills. On the way back down, an animal of a kind I'd never seen before ran straight across my path on the forested slope, affording a surprisingly clear view of its shape and markings.

> Long white nose
> runs like a cat
> the fox-bear
>
> Wakakusa
> on the path back down
> remembering the sound of wind

But were you frightened? asked the first person I met back in town, to whom I described what I'd seen. In the days that followed we went around on foot to many of the well-known sights of this old prefectural capital, at one point joining a bus tour of the surrounding region, visiting a long-established and rather grandiose temple in a small town which, at least according to the guide, who was from a nearby village, had once, even before Nara, been the de facto capital of the country. It was the driver of the tour bus who was able to tell me the name of the mysterious animal I'd encountered on the mountain.

Back and forth all morning
dragonflies
rehearsing the battles of the Yamato Plain

Made of broken statues the wall
still sinking
beyond Hideyoshi's vanished castle

Not a pedigreed animal just a usual animal
the tanuki

Not a pedigreed animal just a(n un)usual animal
the tanuki

Anxious in the night, then off again
dreaming of a visit to the Tooth-Regrowing Temple

Holding the camera steady
a heron
not taking off from the temple roof

At the end of a long day
the tour guide still talking
our bus passing through her old hometown

Hakuin's sermon in the museum
ten words long
still untranslated

That evening we went wandering along the old hill-paths at the edge of town, through an area of open-air shrines. Stone foxes crowded together with tablets to the dead, along with clouds of famished mosquitoes, undeterred by the few incense sticks left burning resolutely here and there – though we came across no other people. I was reminded of a feeling I'd had before, as a child, listening to Japanese tales in translation, read to me by my mother. Later, encountering some of the poetry and novels on my own, I wondered, as I read them, whether I might one day visit the source of such tales myself. In fact the opportunity came, not once but twice, after my mother had become ill, when I found it impossible to travel far from her. This trip, though belated, was the lucky third chance. Nara was the first of Japan's official capitals; the second was not only correspondingly larger but by far the more celebrated of the two. From Nara, Kyoto was suddenly no distance at all.

One father one mother
sweet peas
ragged along the roadside

Another life
ten days of rain and now
in every corner of the world crude sunshine

Arriving in Kyoto, sitting down to organize our time there, it occurred to me that the first Japanese novel I'd read, back in the days when a great enthusiasm for literary translation was just beginning to flourish, had been set in Kyoto. Thus Mishima's *Temple of the Golden Pavilion*, or rather the temple itself, became the natural first stop on our itinerary. Deliberately burnt down in the mid-twentieth century by one of the resident monks – the basis, quite factual, for the plot elaborated in the novel – the pavilion that lent the temple its name had long since been fully restored, even down to the gold leaf reapplied periodically to the outward-facing walls. This building, which had once blazed in my imagination as the centre of a world I might never see, now stood before us, wavering in and out of the confines of its own reflection.

Pure gold
pure reflection
the Golden Pavilion

the Golden Pavilion
burnt down and rebuilt
every moment in the waves

Perched above its own small lake, it seemed to beg comparison to some fabulous water bird, or the legendary phoenix re-emerging from the flames, except for the effect of the gold leaf, which, contrary to expectations, and in contrast with the solid greens and yellows of the neighbouring trees and grasses, was of such translucent fragility that it appeared almost reddish in colour – a form of wealth without grandeur, or of beauty without anti-climax. Afterwards we found a small restaurant where we could try the local summer specialty: buckwheat noodles, served cold, in wooden boxes.

Cool as a cucumber
the cucumbers
in their summer dishes

The restaurant was crowded with other diners, all of them dressed in business clothes and well practised at eating and drinking their way through the lunch rush without the slightest wasted effort. Wherever we strolled in the city or rested for a while, what most caught my eye, the details most at odds with my expectations, were those places meant to be overlooked but nonetheless tended by an invisible someone to whom the task had apparently been assigned – the gently raked ground around the base of a tree on a public street, the corner of an eave where a spider had begun its own self-appointed task of reconstructing the web so recently swept away.

In their weed garden
even the moonlight
painted by snails

It's a truism of a certain way of seeing that the self must first be subtracted from whatever one sees. But could the self somehow be subtracted from one's life in the same way – without losing that life, that is? If so, might not everyday life yet be revealed as a kind of ultimate form? The old wooden guardians, deeply cracked but still fearsome, we'd been studying in various temple alcoves would likely each have had a different answer to this question.

Night after night
before the gods of hell, in consultation
this person I've never met

Flowering on a hillside far from home
whose ghost is this
the chartreuse flowers of the sourgrass

All morning feeling at a loss
and now
the daylight moon

The old pond
fish dozing
somewhere between poems

How stupid!
Longing to be like others
who have gone before me

Whatever private motives may have first led to their construction, the gardens of Kyoto are now said by some to be precisely those places where one might step aside from one's usual life. First a fee must be paid, the ticket received, and only then, bowing briefly, can one pass through the entry gate. Once inside the garden proper, like as not, an elderly woman, habitually stooped, hunched even now on hands and knees, busy grooming the garden floor between three-inch-high shrubs planted in a diamond pattern, will stop to ask you where you're from, beam at your answer, then continue her work with a pair of miniature secateurs and a whisk. Up and down among mossy rocks, here following a stream, there stepping over stepping stones.

> Retracing our steps this way and that
> only to find the lost hat
> neatly folded on a lacquered railing

There comes a time when the places you've lived, the people you've known, do not belong to you, though everything you've experienced is in you, persists in you, and nowhere else in the world. If one or two ghosts or other lonely spirits can still be said to remain among us, perhaps it is only that they are unwilling to abandon us here. It was some days since the last rain had fallen and a few leaves on the path ahead had just begun to stir. A crow called out sharply, and at once, from some distance off, came an answering call, and then another, then another. I looked up. The last sunlight was painted on the pines. My friend, having regained his hat, had already walked on, and now stood waiting for me to follow.

Tide gliding in
over sea-stones
up ahead Osaka Bay

Hidden how long
in the long grass far from home
tonight's moon

From this moment on
among the pines
the real travelling begins

BAXTER'S GRAVE

Palmerston North to Wanganui,
then up the river road.

On to the grave,
which talk has turned

to briars and brambles
to keep it off the maps,

and you the ragged man of God,
or else the god of ragged men.

"Baxter . . . ?" they'll say when asked the way,
although your house still stands.

Broad as daylight
on a bed of river stones.

You're working on a hard new poetry.
I'm on my way to becoming no one –

Palmerston North to Wanganui,
then up the river road,

past elder apples,
and the crumbling gown of Mary.

Futile, though the road leads there.

The New Zealand poet James K. Baxter (1926–1972) is buried in the tribal ground of the Ngati Hau at Jerusalem, a small community in the back country of the North Island, some distance inland along the Wanganui River. After some initial difficulties, and through the help of a friend (the New Zealand physicist who'd first introduced us to Baxter's work), we'd managed to obtain permission from his widow to visit Baxter's grave. Rather than driving the narrow unsealed road ourselves, we'd taken the Mail Coach, which makes deliveries up and down that road. People along the route can leave notes for the driver, who is even willing to pick up groceries in town, delivering them the next day. Along the way we spotted a mailbox with the name Poutini, instantly recognizable from Baxter's poems. In Jerusalem the church hostel was closed for repairs, but we were permitted to look in and wander about. Several dolls had been lain down to sleep in one of the beds, with a coverlet up to the eyes to keep the dust off. We left with a jar of apple jelly made by the nuns. A short muddy path through the brambles led to a small private home whose owner sat working on the front porch. Having washed our hands, we were allowed to enter the adjoining paddock, where we found the gravesite, neatly tended, and on the grave itself, a large river rock, painted entirely white.

for Sharon Thesen

To lie in splendour and decline
on a yellow chaise

and think of nothing
the origins of success and failure

as the rain comes down
though no one watches

and the cool petals
climb out of the twig-tips

into the rain
medallion and trailing vine

thinking: *empires of autumn, the pale pools at Ostia*
filling with silt for a thousand years –

It would have been sometime in the 1990s, I think, when I walked with
a friend into the house on Kitchener and saw for the first time the
elegant chaise longue Sharon had come across in a storefront window
in Montreal and (as she said) had to have, and so had shipped all the
way to East Vancouver, where its yellow satin brocade shed more light
than the sun. And I thought: if only one could lie here ... shortly after
which a few lines began to form themselves. That this particular piece
of furniture has stayed in my mind ever since, and that these lines

have never had a home till now, makes me think, watching a robin (now that it is spring) endlessly pick up and drop a piece of tissue half again her size, that there are many forms of patience.

TO GO TO HUANGSHAN

It's a commonplace in China to say that once you've seen Huangshan (the Yellow Mountain, in Anhui province), you'll be disappointed in any other mountain. Many watercolours, showing twisted limestone peaks engulfed in mist, once thought by Westerners to represent the fantasies of Chinese artists, in fact depict Huangshan. As much as the mountain itself, it is this combination – the shifting view of peaks variously obscured, or clear, or half-obscured by mist – that forms the central image of Huangshan. For centuries, to reach the top, one made the long climb up one of the flights of stone stairs carved into the mountain's sides. Nowadays, though a number of modern hotels have been constructed there, most visitors arrive in the morning by cable car, spend the day wandering among the peaks, and then descend again by cable car before dinner-time. Whether one plans to stay the night or not, it is impossible to be sure in advance of seeing any particular feature of Huangshan. In fact, with the ever-shifting mists, it's hard to say, at any given point, if one has actually succeeded in seeing Huangshan at all.

To go to Huangshan
even in the rain,

for a day and a night and a day,
though you can't know where you are

with the rain and the mist
and the dripping pine-tips –

but a fog-bound bee
and a dragonfly

and a long-necked insect
perch in sequence on the same dripping pine-tip

as if embodiment were jewellery
to be worn by the wearer.

To go to Huangshan
with the crowds and the mist

and then the crowds again
with their useless walking sticks

their caps and flags
and identical raincoats

and friendliness, and greediness,
on something like a forced march, or a party,

but when Huangshan opens its coat
there is nothing that is not a mountain

worn by jewels that are mountains,
maybe death can be defined

as that moment when you are no longer thinking
about returning to Huangshan.

But going to Huangshan
is only half the problem,

the other half
is getting back,

the mountain is always moving,
it is more alive than you are,

seventy-two peaks and twenty days
of bright weather,

more days in the year
than your mind can be said to be clear,

but the mind of Huangshan
is neither your mind nor the mind

of literature,
literature is a country that swallows its dead.

And so to go to Huangshan
though there's not much to see,

seventy-two peaks,
supposedly,

hidden in fickle rain
and impossible mist,

some earlike orchids,
a sleeping bee,

but when the crowds move off
to witness another invisible sunrise

you can hear the mist moving,
the evening squirrel

turns out to be the morning squirrel,
the rat that lives by the restaurant

saunters at ease
past the sleeping staff,

was it envy
or marvel I understood then,

the thing that forces distinctions
then blurs them,

gives mountains a name
then steals their form –

literature deals in nothing
if not names,

your own, for instance,
which exists

in the larger
register of human sounds.

Now every morning I wake before daylight
and wait for the sunrise

to ignite those mists
wherever I am.

Maybe this is the point
of going to Huangshan:

to go on
for as long as you possibly can,

wearing your identical raincoat
of flammable plastic

like a jewel.

Infinite world
recondite world

sad lights and all the rest
unmoored

why make of the world
a world

unless
in the burning blue flowers of June

and if
such a world

why then
such a world

rabbit-haunted
crow-fledged

recondite
pure and empirical

empirical as the burning blue flowers of June
in the yellow of September

and what
in this world

in the burning blue flower
of the world

uninterruptible as rain
in the onion-scented woods

and rabbit-haunted paddocks
of infinite June

is it for
this burning blue rain

in the June of the world

≈

To make
to make

to make of the world
a world

trash rack
and silt trap

the great garlands
of invisible things

grasses and cities
caught there

bookfuls of wild cool air
the hiss of the weir

enough beauty
in the days

the gravel paths
and lolloping dogs

cabbage whites climbing
the invisible spires

the many moods
and pleasures of the river

all ordinary
unpunishable things

then why
why make

why make such a world
sings the blackbird

long before
dawn

long before dawn and the rain coming down

≈

In the liquid hours
of the last night of spring

before the world
pure

unimpeded
turns inside the world

long before the dawn
and summer

and the horses
of summer

chestnut-eyed
fly-haloed

June
to September

whose only labour
is to look

who wakes
who wakes

who wakes in the worn
woods of the world sings the blackbird

high on Bucks Hill
sings the blackbird

unmoored
sings the blackbird

infinite
unimpeded

blackness out of blackness
so

sings the blackbird

≈

Hour sliding
inside hour

season within season
cylindrical

so too each day
each with its autumn

each hour
its own June

as the path
falls by the river

and the river
shifts

cliff-edge to
knife-edge

in the slow
erosion

and remaking of the world
who looks

for what is lost
finds loss

who looks for something other
finds another year

one
inside the other

and the robin
small beneath the hedge

small
reddening the day

and just the one of him

≈

A continent of clouds
or else a city by the river

seen from afar
whiteness and greyness

astray on the water
a thing that falls

silent
each autumn's year

stairways of acorns
and oak leaves

carved on the air
all the tropes spent

and the wind
intransigent

a churchyard for the robin
and the blackbird's cathedral

one half for the living
one half for emptiness

demons in the stone
and bread for the animals

a word
or else a world

for each of them
a monument to clouds

caught in the mirroring water
a bastion for morning glories

a script of broken crockery
unread but beautiful

in the traveller's hour

≋

Whose lights these are
any longer

who can tell
only the new lambs

climbing the fells
and the rills descending

who looks
in old books

any longer
in which ·

it is written
whose house

whose lights
whose lambs

these are
who reads

such histories now
and so

can say
whose land

whose life
whose thoughts these are

climbing the fells
only the rills descending

as if in a woodcut
one page fallen from an old book

long since out of print
and the newly

invited lambs

≈

That someone might wake
not knowing

which river
or which city

which world
this might be

might wake up
in the small hours unashamed

wind in the keyhole
key in the door

not knowing which
which river or which city or which world

might wake as from a
long sleep

twenty years
or fifty

who can tell
wind in the keyhole

key in the door
hearing the rain

that falls upon
Bucks Hill

might wake
still in the small hours

to the sound of rain
clear-headed

as the rain that falls
not knowing

either the sound or the hour

≋

Green fire
alight along the branches

thankless November
and the holly berries

red again
the dusk of

thanklessness
of dashing rain

or failing light
November's ending

and the holly's
green fire

berries
now aloof among the boughs

then why
why make

why make
of the world once more

in the worn woods
of the world once more

in the reticent
hours

and leeward of the rain once more
that falls upon Bucks Hill

unseen
unheard

that green fire once more
burning

in the countless endings of November

≈

To read again
by the lights of the city

lights
reflected in the windows of the past

a stone wall
towering above the river

morning star or
evening star

the many facets
facing west

solid with
pink but fading light

to read again unmoored
as if inside the blackbird's song

clear
unadorned

while overhead
the sky begins to darken

not quite swallowing
the city

and some other life begins
to read that is

although with difficulty
in that fading light

the names of rivers
faces other cities

stone walls that may yet be to be found
strung out along that river

on its short course to the sea

– Durham, 2007, along the River Wear

Most of the places encountered in this book are named and accounted for in the poems in which they occur. Mentioned in passing but not named, though perhaps it might have been, is the cathedral in Dunkeld, a smallish town in southern Scotland. The cathedral was built over several centuries, and largely destroyed in 1560 during the Reformation, when all things "Popish" were to be either actively expunged or confiscated, depending on their value and/or portability. In 1600, the chancel portion was repaired and re-roofed, restoring the church to its role as a functioning place of worship, but the nave portion was left in ruins. Since that time, through various battles and upheavals, it has been maintained in this state, one half for the living, one half, its grasses underfoot, unroofed and open to the sky.

If time, as many have claimed, is a river, then time I suppose must also assume, on occasion, the other shapes of water: snowflake, fog, the melting and reforming cliffs of the polar regions, whirlpools and waterfalls, a surging sea, the running brook in which a book speaks its mind, an oxbow lake. It so happens that the River Braan, at eleven miles in length surely one of the shorter rivers in Scotland and a tributary of the River Tay, which runs scenically past Dunkeld with its half-ruined cathedral, traverses a property once owned by the successive Dukes of Atholl. In the eighteenth century a folly was built here, called Ossian's Hall. Ossian was an invention of the literary mastermind James McPherson, whose "translations" from the work of the third-century Scots-Gaelic bard are often credited with inciting the Romantic movement in literature, thus showing not only that literature makes little distinction between the living and the invented, but that, like water, it must make its own way in response to the contours of its changing environs. The painter Turner and the poet Wordsworth are counted among those who visited here, Wordsworth studiously penning the lines

> And, when the moment comes, to part
> And vanish by mysterious art

halfway through his poem "Effusion," which recounts his visit to the folly and the falls beyond.

Thanks to Kim Maltman, companion on these travels.

And thus we came to it, the falls' vertiginous
chain-mail welded in spume and walking
a cream-coloured column atop black basalt
now black now red in the standing wave
with living fish flashing upwards and backwards
upended in the din still climbing stranded
in volumes no night no day neither
handhold nor footprint just that continuous falling
not one of them made its way through
as we stood and looked down from the precipice
all silver and steam and the wind-borne mist pricking our faces
whether luck or necessity necessity or folly
now held us: *Enter it* said the river's falling
enter it and entered instead its thunderous names.

ACKNOWLEDGEMENTS

Parts and/or versions of these poems have previously appeared in *The Capilano Review, CV2, Descant, Exile, The Literary Review of Canada, The Malahat Review, Matrix, Moosehead, The Walrus,* and *The Warwick Review.*

This book was produced with the support of the Canada Council for the Arts, the City of Toronto through the Toronto Arts Council, and, through the Ontario Arts Council's Writers' Reserve Program, *Arc Poetry Magazine, Brick, Exile,* Brick Books, and Wolsak & Wynn Publishers. Thanks to all.